T0393368

LANGSTON HUGHES

Jazz Poet of the Harlem Renaissance

Celebrating

BLACK ARTISTS

LANGSTON HUGHES

Jazz Poet of the Harlem Renaissance

Enslow Publishing
101 W. 23rd Street
Suite 240
New York, NY 10011
USA

enslow.com

**CHARLOTTE ETINDE-CROMPTON AND
SAMUEL WILLARD CROMPTON**

Published in 2020 by Enslow Publishing, LLC.
101 W. 23rd Street, Suite 240, New York, NY 10011

Library of Congress Cataloging-in-Publication Data

Names: Crompton, Samuel Willard, author. | Crompton-Etinde, Charlotte, author.

Title: Langston Hughes : jazz poet of the Harlem renaissance / Samuel Willard Crompton and Charlotte Etinde-Crompton.

Description: New York : Enslow Publishing, 2020. | Series: Celebrating black artists | Includes bibliographical references. | Audience: Grades 7–12.

Identifiers: LCCN 2018015693| ISBN 9781978503588 (library bound) | ISBN 9781978505339 (pbk.)

Subjects: LCSH: Hughes, Langston, 1902–1967—Juvenile literature. | African American poets—Biography—Juvenile literature. | Poets, American—20th century—Biography—Juvenile literature. | Harlem Renaissance—Juvenile literature. | Harlem (New York, N.Y.)—Biography—Juvenile literature.

Classification: LCC PS3515.U274 Z619 2019 | DDC 818/.5209 [B] —dc23

LC record available at https://lccn.loc.gov/2018015693

Printed in China

To Our Readers: We have done our best to make sure all website addresses in this book were active and appropriate when we went to press. However, the author and the publisher have no control over and assume no liability for the material available on those websites or on any websites they may link to. Any comments or suggestions can be sent by email to customerservice@enslow.com.

Photo Credits: Cover, pp. 3, 88 Underwood Archives/Archive Photos/Getty Images; p. 8 Photo 12/Universal Images Group/Getty Images; p. 11 Everett Historical/Shutterstock.com; pp. 14–15 Niday Picture Library/Alamy Stock Photo; pp. 16, 41, 86 Bettmann/Getty Images; pp. 23, 81 © AP Images; p. 26 Minnesota Historical Society/Corbis Historical/Getty Images; pp. 28–29 Library of Congress/Corbis Historical/Getty Images; pp. 32–33 Library of Congress Prints and Photographs Division Washington, D.C.; pp. 34–35 Michael Ochs Archives/Getty Images; pp. 37, 61, 63 Hulton Archive/Getty Images; p. 45 Culture Club/Hulton Archive/Getty Images; pp. 46–47 Adolf Dehn/Private Collection/Photo © Christie's Images/Bridgeman Images; p. 51 Bill Grant/Alamy Stock Photo; p. 53 Corbis Historical/Getty Images; p. 59 General Photographic Agency/Hulton Archive/Getty Images; p. 67 MPI/Archive Photos/Getty Images; pp. 68–69 Keystone Features/Hulton Archive/Getty Images; pp. 72–73 Hulton Archive/Archive Photos/Getty Images; p. 75 The Protected Art Archive/Alamy Stock Photo; p. 79 Robert W. Kelley/The LIFE Picture Collection/Getty Images; pp. 84–85 Entertainment Pictures/Alamy Stock Photo.

Contents

Kinship and Kingship

Langston Hughes came from what was essentially African American royalty. His mother was descended from an illustrious family that produced a congressman. But kinship was not enough to guarantee ease or comfort. Though he knew about his family's legacy from his earliest days, Langston Hughes grew up with a profound sense of deprivation: financial, material, and familial.

Part of what made Hughes such a charming, and successful, person was his manner of handling difficulties. When other people moaned and lamented, he shrugged and grinned. To be sure, this was part of his charm and part of his disguise. Few people saw beneath the laughter to perceive the pain, and one suspects that is the way Hughes preferred it.

A Challenging Upbringing

Almost every Hughes biography begins with the statement that he was born in Joplin, Missouri, on February 1, 1902.

Langston Hughes was born in 1901.

But the Topeka *Plaindealer*, a prominent African American newspaper, mentioned that "Mrs. Carrie Hughes and her little son Langston are visiting friends in the city before leaving for Buffalo."[1] And the same newspaper ran another social news item with "Little Langston Hughes has been quite ill for the past two weeks. He is improving."[2] Both these articles appeared in the year 1901, suggesting that Hughes's birthdate was somehow mishandled or misplaced. Given that he usually confidently confirmed February 1, 1902, as his birthdate, the chances are that he—and his family—were off by one calendar year, and that February 1, 1901, is the accurate date.

The difference of one year seems small. But the mere fact that the Hughes family got it wrong, and that the mistake was never corrected, suggests the haphazard nature of Langston Hughes's upbringing. He came from proud people who had fallen on hard times.

The Pain of Separation

James Nathaniel Hughes was Langston Hughes's father. A self-made man who had about an equal mixture of African American and Anglo ancestry, James was anything but a devoted father. He abandoned the family when Langston was a baby, moving first to Cuba and then Mexico in search of gainful employment.

Carrie Mercer Langston was Langston's mother. A person of great willpower and undeniable gifts—she wrote poetry and hoped for a career on the stage—she was embittered by her husband's abandonment. Then, too, her dreams and desires were constantly thwarted. Without being too severe, one gains the impression that she was a self-centered mother who saw her son primarily in terms of what he could do for her.

Poor little Langston did not know whether he was coming or going. This was made painfully evident in 1906, when his mother took him on a trip to Mexico to see his father. The hoped-for reconciliation did not take place, and Hughes's only memory of the trip was being carried in his father's arms as the family escaped the wrath of a volcanic eruption.

Langston Hughes knew little but relocation and dislocation in his early years. Soon after they returned from Mexico, Carrie Hughes left her son in the custody of her mother, Mary Leary Langston. This was when Langston was first exposed to the legend of his mother's family.

Grandmother Langston

Mary Leary Langston led a complicated and difficult life. Both African American and Native American, she was born in North Carolina but moved to Ohio in her teenage years. There, she met and married Lewis Sheridan Leary, an ambitious and impulsive young black man who was entranced by the ideas of the radical abolitionist John Brown.

Leary joined John Brown's ill-fated raid on the federal arsenal at Harpers Ferry, Virginia, in 1859. He was one of the first men killed in the fighting. Later that year, the bloodstained shawl Lewis wore was brought to Oberlin, Ohio, and presented to his widow. Langston Hughes first saw the shawl as a young boy, and it made such a profound impression that later he made certain to secure it: he kept it in a bank vault for many years.

John Brown's Raid

In October 1859, John Brown led twenty-one men in an attack on the federal arsenal at Harpers Ferry, Virginia. They seized and held the central part of the facility for almost forty-eight hours before being attacked and overwhelmed by a detachment of US Marines (led by none other than Colonel Robert E. Lee). Wounded, captured, and brought to trial, John Brown defended his actions in court. He did all this to free the black slaves, Brown said, and he would do it again, given the choice. He was found guilty of treason and hanged in December 1859. Many northern whites deplored Brown's use of violence. At the same time, they quietly admired his vigor and resolve, which played a large role in bringing on the Civil War of 1861–1865.

Langston's grandmother, Mary Leary Langston, was once married to an activist who died in the famous Harpers Ferry raid.

Langston Hughes was certainly influenced by his grandmother, who was extremely proud of having been first the wife of Lewis Sheridan Leary and then the wife of Charles Henry Langston, a longtime political activist who worked for equal rights and access to education for black men and women in Ohio and Kansas. But this family prominence did not lead to ease, or even compassion. By the time Langston Hughes went to live with his grandmother, she was an embittered and rather silent person.

Hughes grew up with a strong sense of destiny. He knew of Leary and the Langston family lineage. Very likely, he felt some pressure, a need to live up to this august legacy. But how could he do so with a father in Mexico, an absentee mother, and a grandmother who sat in her rocking chair, grimly thinking about events half a century in the past? Even though the women in his life did not always exercise the best judgment, from his earliest days,

On the Move

Almost everyone who has a family is influenced by that family. And the great majority of people grow up repeating the successes and failures of their parents. In Langston Hughes's case, this led to a life of being perpetually on the move. He may have lived in six different houses before he was ten years old. Later in life, even when he was financially comfortable, Hughes would be on the road.

Langston saw women acting as leaders, with the men in his family almost totally missing.

In 1915, when Langston was fourteen, his grandmother died. His mother and her new husband, Homer Clark, were married around this time, and Langston was again on the move. By that year, this adolescent was beginning to grow up.

In the few photographs that survive, the viewer sees a constantly grinning Langston Hughes. He is the comedian of the family and plays his part well. There is an uplifted eyebrow and a mouth that suggests mirth but also mockery.

The laughter and carefree attitude were completely necessary. Without those qualities, Langston would not have survived his rough childhood. Plenty of other challenges lay before him, and he would meet them with the same studied indifference, the attitude that declared that life is a fool's game and only a fool takes it seriously.

Poems of the Oppressed

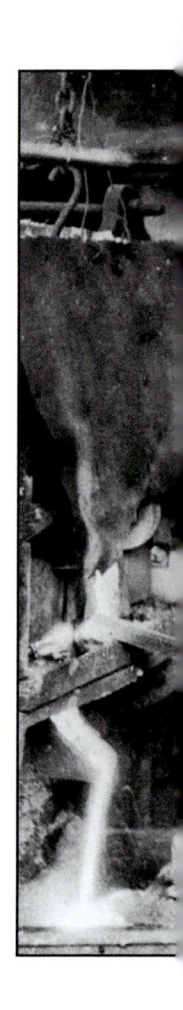

Langston Hughes did not set out to become a poet. Rather, he was called to the work by a combination of circumstances. One of his earliest poems, dating from his high school years, deals with a subject close to his heart—the plight of the common working man:

> The mills
> That grind and grind,
> That grind out steel
> And grind away the lives
> Of men—
> In the sunset their stacks
> Are great black silhouettes
> Against the sky.
> In the dawn
> They belch red fire.
> The mills—
> Grinding new steel,
> Old men.[1]

Langston Hughes was particularly interested in the struggles of mill workers.

The poem was personal. Langston had not yet spent much time working (in time he would) but he already saw what the mills did to people like his stepfather. While the work paid relatively well, it came at great physical cost. His stepfather, Homer Clark, like the great majority of men and women (African Americans especially), had little choice

World War I changed the United States in many ways, including demographically, as men and women from a devastated Europe immigrated to America.

in becoming a machinist in a steel mill. One either labored in a sweatshop or mill, as the factories were called, or one went without food. But even at this tender age, Langston Hughes was already confident of not being called to this type of work. He would do it when necessary, but his eyes were set on something higher.

Finding Friends

By the age of fifteen, Langston had been through a great deal of change and relocation. His high school years, spent with his mother and stepfather in Cleveland, Ohio, were quite an improvement. His mother remained temperamental, and sometimes demanding, but Langston liked his stepfather well enough and was very pleased to have a new stepbrother. More than a decade separated Langston from his stepbrother, Kit, but they became fast friends.

Kansas and Missouri were now far behind. Hughes arrived in Cleveland at an exciting, and rather optimistic, time. The town on the lake, as many called it, experienced boom times during the First World War. The factories increased their workloads, and for a time even the average factory hand made a decent living. A political excitement—a fever almost—overtook the city when America entered World War I in April 1917.

Cleveland's Central High School was full of foreigners, the children of recent immigrants from war-torn Europe. Langston made friends with many of them and was known as one of the most easygoing, adaptable students at Central High. Exposure to Italians, Irish, Poles, and Jews persuaded Langston that the world was filled with minorities and underdogs. African Americans had it worst of all, but there was no reason for them not to reach out to other downtrodden groups:

> My best pal in high school was a Polish boy named Sartur Andrzejewiski. His parents lived in the steel mill district. His mother cooked wonderful cabbage in sweetened vinegar. His rosy-cheeked sisters were named Regina and Sabina. And the whole family had about them a quaint and kindly foreign air, bubbling with hospitality. They were devout Catholics, who lived well and were very jolly.[2]

Langston had grown up in the very Protestant heartland, the Trans-Mississippi Midwest. His early experiences at the local Baptist church had not been positive. He loved his new foreign friends at Central High and secretly envied their family comforts, but he wanted no part of Roman Catholicism, or any other religion.

Three things called to Langston Hughes during his teenage years: friends, athletics, and writing. The friendship part came naturally to him, and he adopted the carefree, innocent style that kept him so photogenic, radiating from within him, well into middle age. Athletics were more challenging, but he became a skilled member of the high school track team. And his writing began to flourish, as seen in the poem "When Sue Wears Red":

> When Susanna Jones wears red
> Her face is like an ancient cameo
> Turned brown by the ages.
>
> Come with a blast of trumpets,
>   Jesus!
> When Susanna Jones wears red

> A queen from some time-dead Egyptian night
> Walks once again.
>
> Blow trumpets, Jesus!
> And the beauty of Susanna Jones in red
> Burns in my heart a love-fire sharp like pain.
> Sweet silver trumpets.
>   Jesus![3]

The emotions are not surprising—they have been felt by millions of teenagers, before and since. But the expression is first-rate. Langston already knew how to use color to create a striking and memorable visual, and he made the reader believe in this high school beauty.

Internalized Racism

African Americans of the early twentieth century knew the deeply damaging effects of racial slurs all too well. But these were nothing compared to the minstrel shows that dominated early 1900s theatre. Minstrelsy involved white actors wearing makeup–or "blackface"– to make themselves appear to be black men and women. The actors would then mock and caricature African Americans as lazy, unscrupulous, and unintelligent. Not only did this reinforce the racist attitudes of a white-dominated society, but unfortunately, it also often shaped how black men and women viewed themselves. Self-hatred sometimes became a means of coping with the anger or abuse that was a major part of institutional racism.

The Father Returns

In the spring of 1919, Langston Hughes received a brief telegram from his father. James Nathaniel Hughes had not written to his son in years, but he now explained that he was in New York City and would soon return to Mexico. Langston should be ready to meet him at the train depot.

The telegram produced more joy, even elation, than sadness. Langston Hughes felt half-abandoned by his mother, who frequently left town with his stepfather and stepbrother. There was a period when the high school student rented an attic and completely took care of his own needs. The idea of seeing Mexico produced plenty of excitement. Years later, Hughes described the first meeting:

> The hotel was on Central Avenue, a block and a half from the restaurant where my mother worked as a waitress. I began to walk down Central Avenue as fast as I could. When I was about three blocks above the hotel I saw a little-bronze man with a moustache, coming rapidly up the street toward me. We looked closely at each other as we passed. Then we turned and looked back.
>
> The man said: "Are you Langston?"
>
> I said: "Yes. Are you my father?"
>
> "Why weren't you at the train last night?" he asked.
>
> "We moved, and I didn't get your wire till this morning."
>
> "Just like n******," he spat out. "Always moving!"[4]

While the n-word is often used as a term of affection in twenty-first century African American discourse, it became apparent to Langston that his father really meant the word as a slur or curse: his father hated his own people. There was something particularly bitterly ironic about this, as James Hughes had relocated to Mexico—and started the entire family down a path that ended in their separation—because he thought he would have a better chance of succeeding outside of America, which, he believed, would never treat a black man fairly.

Chapter 3

Rivers and Oceans

The summer of 1919 was a miserable time for Langston Hughes. Previously, he imagined his father as a tough but handsome and cheerful cowboy. Instead, he was stuck with a grouchy, grumpy, and very dollar-conscious businessman.

James Nathaniel Hughes and his son had almost nothing in common. Langston liked to lounge in bed all morning, while his father was forever up and out in the world. James had come a long way. He owned a ranch and other properties that came to over $60,000 in value. But he was far from content:

> My father hated Negroes...I think he hated himself, too, for being a Negro. He disliked all his family because they were Negroes and remained in the United States, where none of them had a chance to be much of anything...My father said he wanted me to leave the United States as soon as I finished high school, and never return—unless I wanted to be a porter or a red cap all my life.[1]

Of course, what James declared was undeniably true: African Americans had an extraordinarily difficult time

Langston Hughes's shyness and sensitivity come through in this photograph of him as a teenager.

in twentieth-century America. What Langston Hughes objected to was his father's confusing and unreasoning hatred of practically all his own people.

Sojourn in Mexico

Mexico contains much natural beauty, and Langston could have enjoyed his time there. But his father was forever urging, even demanding, that he hurry up—whether it was with his horseback riding, his Spanish lessons, or his mathematics and accounting. The summer turned into an ordeal, with Langston wishing to escape.

On one occasion, his father planned to take him to Mexico City to see a bullfight. The morning of their planned departure, Langston came down with a terrible sickness that prevented him from making the trip. His father went anyway, and on return he had to take Langston to a hospital. Langston may well have suffered from a serious illness. One suspects, however, that the sickness was also a way to escape being in his father's presence. By the time he returned to Cleveland, for his final year of high school, Langston had shaken off whatever illusions that he had entertained about his father. The truth was far less romantic, and more severe.

Graduation and Inspiration

Langston did not find matters much better back home in Cleveland. His mother and his stepfather were at odds, and the household was not happy. Langston concentrated on his studies and was proud to graduate in the spring of

1920 with honors. He said farewell to the many friends he had made.

Given his developing literary skill, Langston should have attended college. He was not certain of his goal, however, and there was no money for a fancy school such as Columbia University, where some of his friends were headed. Langston, therefore, surprised almost everyone by saying he would go to Mexico again: he hoped to persuade his father to finance his education. Carrie Hughes Clark was as astonished as anyone. She complained that her son was leaving just when he might amount to something and help the family. But Langston went, just the same. And on that journey, he received the inspiration for one of his finest poems:

> I've known rivers:
> I've known rivers ancient as the world and
>   older than the flow of human blood in
>   human veins.
>
> My soul has grown deep like the rivers.
>
> I bathed in the Euphrates when dawns
>   were young.
> I built my hut near the Congo and it lulled
>   me to sleep.
> I looked upon the Nile and raised the
>   pyramids above it.
> I heard the singing of the Mississippi when
>   Abe Lincoln went down to New Orleans,
>   and I've seen its muddy bosom turn all
>   golden in the sunset.
> I've known rivers:

The Mississippi River served as an inspiration for Hughes's "The Negro Speaks of Rivers."

Ancient, dusky rivers.

My soul has grown deep like the rivers.[2]

Hughes wrote "The Negro Speaks of Rivers" as his railway car crossed the Mississippi, headed for Texas and then Mexico. Many other poets and writers of prose (perhaps thousands in all) had taken similar trips, passing over that same section of the Midwest, but Langston Hughes was the first, and perhaps the most successful, to capitalize on what he saw. Plenty of other poems would come to his fertile brain, but very few would be quite as poignant as this one.

Renewed Conflict

Arriving in Toluca, Mexico, Hughes found his father unchanged. James N. Hughes was as hard-driving and unsympathetic as before. Being nineteen and a high school graduate made a difference, however. On this visit, Langston was able to compete with his father, and even to acquire some laurels. He taught English to a group of Mexican men and women, challenged his father's ideas about what constituted the good life, and had the immense pride of seeing his poem "Rivers" published in *The Crisis*, a prominent New York periodical written by and for African Americans.

James was surprised to see his son's name on the contributor page of *The Crisis*, but he shrugged it off, asking only how long it had taken to write and how much money it was worth. Father and son were already at loggerheads, but this conversation pointed them straight in the direction of separation yet again.

Langston worked up his courage and asked his father to pay for his expenses at Columbia University. James N.

Fresh Perspective

Many young people want to write, and many try their hand at it. Why did young Langston Hughes succeed where so many others failed? Hughes never addressed this question directly, but the modern reader suspects that his lifestyle, particularly his frequent moves, had a lot to do with success. Hughes was always ready to try something new—a new home, friend, or situation—and the freshness of his unique experience allowed his writing to flourish.

In 1921, Langston Hughes left Mexico to pursue his education in New York City.

Hughes was not completely against the idea. He believed his son could profit from an education, but it needed to be practical. The father agreed to pay the son's expenses, as long as Hughes enrolled to study geology.

This was not what Langston Hughes had in mind. He had a practical bent, too, however. If his father would only pay for a practical education, then that was what he would try. And in the autumn of 1921, he left Mexico—and his father—and headed to New York City.

The ocean voyage from Veracruz was Hughes's first major trip at sea (there would be many others). Hughes endured all sorts of discomforts, but to him they were all made worth it when he saw New York City from the harbor. He knew he was experiencing the same anticipation and excitement as millions of immigrants who had arrived on its doorstep, full of hope for the future:

But, boy! At last! New York was pretty, rising out of the bay in the sunset—the thrill of those towers of Manhattan with their million golden eyes, growing slowly taller and taller above the green water, until they looked as if they could almost touch the sky! Then Brooklyn Bridge, gigantic in the dusk!....All this made me feel it was better to come to New York than to any other city in the world.[3]

Student and Sailor

Langston Hughes arrived in New York City and quickly settled in Harlem, a growing section of the city that was rapidly becoming home to many African Americans, especially those involved in the arts. His first rented room was at a YMCA, and it was that kind of peripatetic existence that marked his life for the next decade.

The Beauty of Harlem

Hughes was admitted to Columbia University, one of the finest of Ivy League schools. He was one of a small number of African American students. But the academic life did not appeal to Hughes. He spent as much time in Harlem, observing street scenes and patronizing nightclubs, as he did at his studies. One can fault him for wasting time, but Hughes was adamant: he wanted to taste life directly, not only learn of it through books.

James N. Hughes had promised to fund his son's education, but the checks he sent were almost always late.

While Hughes was fascinated by the vibrant atmosphere of Harlem, his studies at Columbia University (*pictured*) were far less interesting.

Langston lived, therefore, with both the sense that school was unimportant and that he might hear a knock at the door of a university official evicting him from the premises. But along with the insecurity of his days, there was the excitement of his nights. Hughes simply loved Harlem.

In the spring of 1922, Hughes gave up on his education. He had earned decent, though not spectacular, grades, and

there was a good chance that the mining career his father envisioned for him would come about. But Hughes was bored with school and completely disenchanted with his father. Leaving Columbia after only one year, Hughes lived by his wits, taking up all sorts of work—he even worked on a Staten Island farm for a few months. But his real desire was to go away to sea.

Going to Sea

In the autumn of 1922, Hughes signed aboard a ship and discovered—to his complete surprise—that it was not going out to sea. Rather, this ship headed up the Hudson River to Jones Point, just below the US Military Academy at West Point. Hughes was bitterly disappointed at first, but his poetry clearly benefited from the months spent in isolation—he wrote some of his finest poems, like the famous "Mother to Son," during that lonely winter.

Not until 1923 did Hughes get aboard another ship and out to sea. This time, he coordinated his energies and went aboard a freighter headed for the west coast of Africa. He could hardly believe his good luck—he was shipping out to see the land of his ancestors and being paid a modest amount for the experience.

Africa was an eye-opener for Langston Hughes. He thrilled to see the coastline, the villages, and the people with whom he identified. There was some sadness,

Harlem would become a haven for Hughes as he pioneered jazz poetry.

however, as he later admitted in his autobiography. Hughes expected the African people to claim him as one of their own. Instead they pointed to his copper features and said he was not all black.[1] As Hughes wrote to his closest friend, Countee Cullen:

This is our sixteenth port, Lagos, just where the coast curves south again...We usually anchor out and our cargo is taken by surf boats in charge of eight oars-men whose paddles are three-pointed like Father Neptune's fork and the oars-men themselves gorgeously naked save a whisp of loin-cloth.[2]

Many historians and biographers have called attention to this letter and its depiction of male sensuality. Most of them believe that the letter suggests Hughes was gay, primarily a lover of men. The truth is more complicated. Like his good friend Countee Cullen, Hughes's sexuality has been a source of much speculation for scholars. Cullen married twice, but most readings of his letters suggest that he leaned more strongly toward men. Langston Hughes never married, and this has only fueled the rumor that he was a closeted gay man. While there is no strong consensus about Hughes's sexuality—one biographer has even suggested Hughes was asexual, or uninterested in sexual relationships—there is no doubt that he possessed a deep admiration for other black men. This is likely at least part of the reason that the rejection of his blackness (or lack thereof) in Africa stung so much.

A Famous Friend

No one would predict the strong friendship between Countee Cullen and Langston Hughes. The former was punctilious and precise, while the latter enjoyed fun and pranks. The two young men shared a powerful love of poetry, however, as well as a sense that they, as young literary men, needed to do something for the African American cause. Like Langston Hughes, Countee Cullen experienced a difficult and insecure childhood: he now lived with his foster parents in a massive church rectory in Harlem. Some of Hughes's happiest hours were spent visiting with the Cullen family.

Nonetheless, Hughes made it back to America safe and sound and happier than he had been in years. The African sunshine did him good, as did witnessing tribal people leading simple, more natural lives. Once back in New York, Hughes stayed only a short time before shipping out on another freighter. This time Holland was the destination.

Arriving in Rotterdam and disgusted with the ship captain's discipline, Hughes jumped ship and caught a train to Paris. In his letters, there is no sense of shame for having abandoned his ship and fellow sailors; rather, Hughes feels a powerful sense of destiny. He *must* see the City of Light!

Though Hughes initially was excited to travel to Paris, he was disappointed by the lack of courtesy and kindness he found there.

A Disappointment in Paris

Keeping body and soul together was much more difficult than Hughes imagined. Though he was accustomed to living on the margins of American society, to going without many material things, he was appalled and even angry by the lack of comfort and charity in Paris. He wrote Countee Cullen:

> Kid, stay in Harlem! The French are the most franc-loving, sou-clutching, hard faced, hard-worked, cold and half-starved set of people I've ever seen in life. Heat—unknown. Hot water—what is it? You even pay for a smile here. Nothing, absolutely nothing is given away. You even pay for water in a restaurant, or the use of the toilette. And do they like Americans of any color? They do not!!![3]

Many other Americans tourists quietly said similar things. In the 1920s, Paris was a rather sad and drab imitation of the gaiety known prior to the First World War. Hughes was in an especially tight spot, however. Like any American with a case of wanderlust, he was expected to like—even adore—Paris. As an African American artist, he was expected to fall on his knees and say Paris was the best. But Hughes was scrupulously honest where opinion is concerned. He could not hide the painful truth, especially not from his dear friend back home in New York. Hughes stayed in Paris several months. He found work as a waiter in a nightclub that featured American music (jazz especially). But he was not sad to bid Paris farewell.

In the company of Dr. Alain Locke, a friend of Cullen, Hughes toured southern France and northern Italy.

Running out of money, Hughes had to stay in the Italian city of Genoa for nearly two months. Virtually without funds and almost completely lacking in friends, Hughes managed to write some fine poems. When he finally caught a ship bound for America, Hughes did not lament going back to the "boring" United States. He had tasted some of the supposedly finer aspects of the European experience and found them lacking.

Sudden Fame

Langston Hughes had already done rather well. At the tender age of twenty-three, he had written many poems, several of which found their way into African American journals such as *The Crisis*. None of these publications prepared Hughes for the sudden fame that came his way in 1925–1926. Thanks to the appearance of his first volume of poetry, and to some outstanding self-publicity, Hughes became better known to the general public, both black and white.

Courting the Famous

For a brief time, Hughes worked as a waiter and busboy in Washington, DC. By an odd twist of fate, the renowned poet Vachel Lindsay dined at the restaurant one evening. Hastily finding—or rescribbling—three of his poems, Hughes left them on Lindsay's table and then fled in embarrassment.

When Lindsay was invited to speak, an hour later, he dwelled for some time on the incident. An unknown black

Just before his rise to fame, Hughes briefly worked as a busboy in a restaurant in Washington, DC.

poet had left poems, Lindsay asserted, and he went on to declare them quite good. When Hughes returned to work the next evening, he found journalists at the restaurant. They were eager to interview and photograph him, and the result was a handsome piece of publicity.

Was Hughes his own best publicist? Sometimes, this seems to be the case. Most people who knew him well declared that even the most obvious form of fame-seeking was acceptable coming from Hughes because he did it with such self-effacement.

The Weary Blues

Though he steered a clear path of independence, Langston Hughes was often fortunate in his friends. Countee Cullen exposed Hughes to a wide range of Harlem's society, and Dr. Alain Locke published several of Hughes's poems in *The New Negro*, Locke's anthology of fiction, poetry, and essays published in 1925. That same year also saw the appearance of Hughes's first book, *The Weary Blues*.

That Hughes had a natural sympathy for the average, common working person was obvious. To this, he added a keen ear for that person's music, obvious in poems like "The Weary Blues":

> Droning a drowsy syncopated tune,
> Rocking back and forth to a mellow croon,
>   I heard a Negro play.
> Down on Lenox Avenue the other night
> By the pale dull pallor of an old gas light
>   He did a lazy sway…
>   He did a lazy sway…
> To the tune o' those Weary Blues.

> With his ebony hands on each ivory key
> He made that poor piano moan with melody.
> O Blues![1]

The blues, a style of music that grew out of black spirituals and work songs, had become quite popular with the average American over the previous decade. Langston Hughes suddenly turned the blues into a literary phenomenon, however, and he upset some staid poetry circles by asking that the blues be played while he recited.

Though "The Weary Blues" is a vibrant expression of Harlem life and art, Hughes goes far beyond his depiction of urban life. In "Lament for Dark Peoples," he expresses ideas about racial oppression that he first acquired in Africa:

> I was a red man one time,
> But the white men came.
> I was a black man, too,
> But the white men came.
>
> They drove me out of the forest.
> They took me away from the jungles.
> I lost my trees.
> I lost my silver moons.
>
> Now they've caged me
> In the circus of civilization.
> Now I herd with the many—
> Caged in the circus of civilizations.[2]

No one could deny that this is not only first-rate poetry; it is also first-rate social commentary. Hughes's interest in black oppression continues in "The Jester," where he examines white society's impulse to cast black citizens in the role of the fool, an object of comedy and ridicule—and the parallel phenomenon of black men and women who internalized this negative image and used humor to deflect their pain:

> In one hand
> I hold tragedy
> And in the other
> Comedy, —
> Masks for the soul.
> Laugh with me.
> You would laugh!
> Weep with me.
> You would weep!
> Tears are my laughter.
> Laughter is my pain.
> Cry at my grinning mouth,
> If you will.
> Laugh at my sorrow's reign.
> I am the Black Jester,
> The dumb clown of the world,
> The booted, booted fool of silly men.
> Once I was wise.
> Shall I be wise again?[3]

The Weary Blues attracted a large audience. Thousands, perhaps tens of thousands, of readers began to regard Langston Hughes as the number-one black poet of his time. Hughes had only one rival: his dear friend Countee Cullen.

Friends and Rivals

Countee Cullen admired Langston Hughes. Unlike his good friend, Cullen was never able to break free from

Hughes had both a treasured friend and a professional rival in
Countee Cullen (1903–1946).

familial and social constraints. Adopted by the Reverend Frederick A. Cullen, Countee felt it necessary, throughout life, to act as a paragon of virtue. He may have wished to go to Africa on a freighter, but he believed it outside of the social norm.

Cullen and Hughes also differed on the fine details of poetry. They agreed that poetry was intended to stir the heart and move the emotions. But how should this be accomplished? By 1925, Hughes had already become a titan of jazz poetry, developing a loose free-flowing style that remained for the rest of his life. Cullen, by contrast, had already brought out his first book of poems, *Color*, but he remained bound to a by-the-book poetic style. In a 1926 issue of *Opportunity*, Cullen reviewed *The Weary Blues*—but his reaction was not entirely positive. He wrote that he regarded "the jazz poems as interlopers in the company of the other truly beautiful poems in other sections of the book," and that there was "too much emphasis on strictly Negro themes."

Hughes had already demonstrated his skill as a poet. But he had yet to make a major statement in prose. This changed with the publication of "The Negro Artist and the Racial Mountain," in *The Nation*.

Hughes begins the essay by lamenting over Countee Cullen, whom he identifies simply as one of the finest black

The rhythms of jazz music played a central role in Harlem's culture and in Langston Hughes's poetry.

poets. Hughes recalls a young black poet, presumably Cullen, saying "I want to be a poet—not a Negro poet."[4] Hughes takes this as a quiet statement of desire: a wish to be white. Hughes goes on to delineate the attitude of the black middle and upper class, filled with people who do not want to be seen as close to "the street" or the daily struggle of millions of African Americans:

> But then there are the low-down folks, the so-called common element, and they are the majority— may the Lord be praised! The people who have their hip of gin on Saturday nights, and are not too important to themselves or the community, or too well fed, or too learned to watch the lazy world go round.[5]

Hughes had identified with these people ever since his peripatetic boyhood. Becoming a twenty-something-year-old poet made the identification even stronger. What especially infuriated the adult Hughes was the middle- and upper-class blacks who would not pay to hear a blues performance or attend black theatre: they thought themselves above it.

> Jazz to me is one of the inherent expressions of Negro life in America, the eternal tom-tom beating in the Negro soul, the tom-tom of revolt against weariness in a white world, a world of subway trains, and work, work, work...Let the blare of Negro jazz bands and the bellowing voice of Bessie Smith singing the blues penetrate the closed ears of the colored near intellectuals...We younger Negro artists who create now intend to express our individual dark-skinned selves without fear or shame.[6]

As a statement of artistic and social purpose, this essay has seldom, if ever, been equaled. Though his friendship with Countee Cullen survived, Hughes's strong words marked a deep schism in their relationship.

Through publication of *The Weary Blues*, Langston Hughes claimed his place as a leading black poet. In his essay "The Racial Mountain," Hughes established himself as even more than an impressive artist: he was a man concerned with racial pride and the advancement of his people.

The Godmother

The peak of Langston Hughes's career was in 1926–1927. He had a fine book of poetry in the bookstores and another inside his mind, almost ready to emerge. Some people were already calling him the finest black poet of the era. But Hughes had not overcome all his doubts and insecurities. His doubts would bear fruit: as he placed his trust in one supposed "savior," he came to regret the decision.

A Freshman Again

In 1926, Hughes entered Lincoln University, the first ever historically black college and university (HBCU), as an undergraduate. He still had credits from his time at Columbia, but it made sense to make a fresh start.

Hughes did not have money for his tuition—this was provided by Amy Springarm, one of a number of generous benefactors who helped him over the years. Hughes settled in for his studies, but a part of his soul remained restless. Hughes often spent four days a week on the college campus in Pennsylvania and hastened to Manhattan, more

After leaving Columbia University, Hughes restarted his studies at Lincoln University.

specifically Harlem, to enjoy the busy nightlife on long weekends. By now, he was a minor celebrity, accustomed to giving readings of his poetry. Perhaps it irritated Hughes that he, a published poet, had to tamely attend classes at Lincoln University, but if so, he concealed his dissatisfaction.

On one of his frequent trips to Manhattan, Hughes was introduced to Charlotte Osgood Mason. Perhaps he already knew that she made a point of subsidizing African American talent; then again, the meeting may have been a pleasant surprise. In either case, Mason soon became Hughes's number-one patron.

Godmother Mason

Charlotte Osgood Mason was a very wealthy white woman who lived on Park Avenue in New York City. Her physician husband had died two decades earlier, leaving her with a large fortune. Like her late husband, Charlotte Mason was a strong believer in psychic and paranormal events. But she also had more mainstream, ostensibly philanthropic, interests.

During the mid-1920s, Charlotte Mason turned her formidable energy to work on behalf of talented African Americans. Previously enamored of Native Americans, Charlotte Mason now believed that black Americans represented the purest, and most enlightened, of all American ethnic groups.

Developing a dream of what she called a "bridge to Africa," Charlotte Mason sought talented African American artists and writers. She was much impressed with Dr. Alain Locke, who became the most longstanding of her "pupils." She admired and sponsored the up-and-coming Zora Neale Hurston, who was a pioneer in the collection of African American folklore. But "Godmother," as she insisted people call her, reserved her greatest admiration and praise for Langston Hughes.

The date of their first meeting is not known. What is certain is that Hughes became her "pet," the favorite among her black pupils. Time and again, Hughes went to her Park Avenue apartment to regale her with poems and stories; time and again, she lavished attention, even love, upon him. For a man in his late twenties who had never enjoyed sufficient maternal affection, Godmother Mason seemed, truly, like a fairy godmother. Then, too, she

Zora Neale Hurston and Langston Hughes became fast friends, but they had a falling out over the authorship of their cowritten play, *Mule Bone*.

sponsored Hughes to the extent of $150 per month, a very attractive sum at the time.

Zora Neale Hurston

The money from Godmother Mason was enough for Hughes to maintain a decent apartment and to care for his mother and his stepbrother, Kit. He also had time and the funds to do a research trip into the southern states. Hughes was appalled by the amount of racism he encountered, but he was charmed to meet—and become fast friends with— Zora Neale Hurston.

Born in Alabama and raised in Florida, Hurston had a stronger claim for understanding the Deep South. She and Hughes came from different social backgrounds, but they thought alike and laughed a great deal (like Hughes, Hurston found life at least as comic as tragic). Both possessed a strong drive to succeed in the literary world and to highlight African American stories in the process.

Hughes and Hurston were just enough alike to appreciate each other's company. Whether either had romantic feelings for the other is still a question, though it's widely assumed that Hurston had some unrequited feelings for Hughes. But there is no doubt they spent several months in each other's company, on an extended research trip through the Deep South. Though Hughes was the surer and more experienced craftsman, turning out poems at a rapid pace, Hurston knew the territory better and her input was invaluable.

Hughes returned from the trip afire with new ideas. He introduced Hurston to Charlotte Mason—and soon Hurston would be Godmother Mason's newest prize pupil.

Though Hurston and Hughes would end their friendship in a dispute over the play they coauthored, *Mule Bone*, the big break was between Hughes and Godmother Mason.

A Difficult Separation

Early in 1930, Godmother Mason demanded more material from Hughes. Accusing him of laziness and taking too much time off, she demanded not only poems but also a detailed work schedule. Hughes balked. While he professed great love for Godmother, both in letters and in person, he was a writer and felt that he needed the freedom to decide what to write and when to write it. Very likely, Hughes believed this was the start of a negotiation and that Godmother would come to her senses. But he did not realize just how controlling and critical his patron could be.

Accustomed to having her way, in a manner that only great wealth can provide, Godmother Mason rebuked Hughes. First she told him off, and then she simply ignored him. Hughes had only wished to gain greater independence from Godmother, so the loss shook him to the core. Charlotte Mason had given him something he received from no other woman. Devastated, Hughes underwent several brief, but intense, illnesses, all of which were likely generated by grief over the loss.

Payback

Hughes waited years to strike back at Godmother Mason. Psychologically, he would have done better to leave the matter alone, but his quick, facile pen allowed him to take vengeance of a sort. In one of his plays, which never

A Powerful Woman

Langston Hughes suffered a great deal in the aftermath of his separation from Godmother Mason. Charlotte Osgood Mason, however, did not seem to experience the same, or similar, feelings. Hughes had been her favorite, the "pupil" that spoke the most to her desire to honor African American culture. But Mason was so used to command, and the power that comes from money, that she recovered quickly. It seems clear, in retrospect, that she relished having control over these promising black artists in a way that went against her image as a philanthropist. She also feuded with Zora Neale Hurston but maintained good relations with Alain Locke to the end of her days.

reached the stage, Hughes created a character clearly based on Mason—an overpowering, demanding, and ultimately selfish person. But his best and most effective words came, as so often, in poetry:

> What right has anyone to say
> That I
> Must throw out pieces of my heart
> For pay?
>
> For bread that helps to make
> My heart beat true,
> I must sell myself
> To you?

A factory shift's better,
A week's meagre pay,
Than a perfumed note asking:
What poems today?[1]

Set Adrift

Cut off from financial help and emotional support, Hughes nearly floundered. Only the opportunity to go south perked up his spirits. He went with Zell Ingram, a Cleveland artist. The two men journeyed down the East Coast. They stopped briefly in Florida, but Cuba was their main hope and destination. Arriving there, Hughes was charmed by the freer society he experienced. Cuba might have been oppressed in a political sense, but culturally its people seemed happier and more expressive.

Despite Hughes's general satisfaction with Cuba, racism still presented a major challenge. Hughes and Ingram were involved in a disturbing episode during which they were denied entry to a beach based on their race. While a judge dismissed the legal complaint brought by the white owners of the beach, by the time they departed Cuba, both men were very happy to be back in the United States.

Hughes was nearly broke when he learned of a new opportunity: a ship was about to sail for the Soviet Union. Believing he might find *one* society where racism was not a prominent factor, Hughes pledged to join the company.

Russia and Spain

Langston Hughes went aboard the ship just an hour before it departed New York. This was typical Hughes style: he specialized in last-minute appearances.

Cold Days in Moscow

The plan that Hughes was involved in was for several African Americans to collectively write and produce a film about black life in the United States. Hughes could tell early on, however, that most of his colleagues were not up to the task—there were almost no filmmakers among them.

Arriving in Joseph Stalin's Russia, the African American artists received a great deal of attention. The leader of a repressive Communist regime, Stalin was delighted to have black Americans view the progress he had made. For his part, Hughes was equally impressed. He found little to no overt racism in the Soviet Union.

Hughes had always been a friend of the workers, the common folk, and this continued during his Russian

Hughes greatly enjoyed the time he spent in Moscow, finding Russia to be a country that appreciated black artists.

sojourn. He was more interested in hearing stories from the workers than in listening to Communist Party debates, for example. As he traveled the western part of the Soviet Union, Hughes remembered the enthusiasm with which he and fellow high school students had greeted the end of World War I and the Russian Revolution that ousted the czar. But the fun and fanfare began to grow thin. Hughes wrote a friend back home:

> I'm afraid you probably think me dead, my silence indicating that I have departed this earth…One

thing that discouraged my writing down there is that the mails are terribly irregular, the camels and trains being equally slow...I have a great deal of interesting material for the book I want to do about the DARK PEOPLE OF THE SOVIETS.[1]

As usual, Hughes was fascinated by the commoners, the down-and-out folk. In the USSR, he found little prejudice against African Americans; but on the other hand, he discovered that the majority of Russians were deeply prejudiced against their compatriots in Central Asia. Hughes had already made one tour of the Black Sea region; he now moved farther, exploring sections of Central Asia.

How Hughes managed all this remains somewhat mysterious. He had almost no money, and the Soviet Union was a vast place. But Hughes employed his unique brand of charm that had previously worked back home, and he usually succeeded. For a time, he traveled in the company of an ardent Communist, Arthur Koestler, but when the two parted ways, Hughes traveled virtually alone. He took the Trans-Siberian Railroad all the way across the Soviet Union, arriving in Vladivostok, on the western side of the Pacific Ocean.

All sorts of friendships developed, and Hughes used the same kind of "here today, gone tomorrow" tactics that he did with romances back home in the United States. Again, the marvel is that he was not resented. Whether they were friends, lovers, or fellow literary types, the people Hughes left lamented his departure but did not hold it against him. About the only part of the journey that was not satisfying, or fun, was Hughes's time in Japan.

Like Hughes, the author and journalist Arthur Koestler had a complicated relationship to working-class issues.

A Change of Heart

Arthur Koestler (1905-1983) was a Hungarian Jew who embraced the Russian Revolution and the Communist Party. He and Langston Hughes made first-rate traveling companions: they both wanted to see, and experience, as much as possible. Koestler was an ardent follower of the Communists at this time; years later, he renounced the Communist Party and wrote *Darkness at Noon*, one of the most poignant books against Stalin and Russian Communism.

Peril in the Pacific

After his time in China, Hughes sailed for Japan, a place he deeply desired to see. But Japan was in the throes of a social and political revolution of its own. Under Emperor Hirohito, Japan had just embarked on an imperialistic program. Hughes was briefly held in prison, and then deported as an undesirable, because his writings displayed a powerful anti-imperialist message.

Once more, Hughes boarded a ship, and this time he arrived in sunny California. He could have headed straight back to New York City, but he spent time with fellow writers in the seaside town of Carmel and developed a lasting fondness for the Golden State. When he did return to Manhattan, he was celebrated as one of the first African Americans to travel around the globe.

In the 1930s, Hughes reported on the Spanish Civil War, a conflict between the Nationalists, led by General Francisco Franco (*pictured*) and a resistance army loyal to the Second Spanish Republic.

When he returned to New York, Langston Hughes was only thirty-four, but he was already *the* literary lion of the African American community. His old friend-turned-rival Countee Cullen had written magnificently in the 1920s, but by 1935, his pen was largely silent. The Jamaican-born Claude MacKay appealed to many black readers, but his fan base was not as large as Hughes's. Five years had passed since Hughes lost the sponsorship of "Godmother" Mason, and he had fully emerged from the shadow of that relationship. What no one—including Langston Hughes—anticipated was that he would soon travel again.

Reporting from the Front Lines

In 1936, Spain was torn apart by a civil war pitting the Republicans against the Nationalists, with General Francisco Franco leading the latter group. The war that developed was a brutal one, in which Franco's forces used airplanes to bomb both military and civilian targets. Appalled by the war's brutality, several thousand Americans joined to form the International Brigade, a group of foreign volunteers assisting the Republicans. Hughes joined them.

But Hughes did not fight. Rather, he was a journalist covering the war. However, his prolonged exposure to the war made it almost inevitable that he would embrace the Republican cause, and argue—with his pen—for their victory. Hughes was friendly with most of the leading Americans of the International Brigade. One is tempted to compare his participation with that of Ernest Hemingway, but the two men were very different, both in character and in their approach to the war. Hughes liked Hemingway quite well, but they did not spend much time together.

As the effort began to fail, Hughes packed and headed for home. As he crossed the border from war-torn Spain to peaceful France, he enjoyed the scenery and the peace, but he had a sense of foreboding. What he—and others—had witnessed in Spain was, indeed, the prelude to the terrible cataclysm of the Second World War. Then, too, Hughes had personal trials to endure.

Simply Himself

Some would say that a person does not become entirely authentically himself (or herself) until his parents depart the scene. This was especially so for Langston Hughes, whose early life was defined by the absence of a typical family unit.

His Father's Death

James N. Hughes died in Mexico in 1936. Langston Hughes was in California, but he went straight to Mexico to pay his respects. When his father's will was read aloud, neither Langston nor his mother were even mentioned. Instead, James divided his property among three Mexican sisters who had cared for him for many years.

In his typical fashion, Langston Hughes neither protested nor lamented the terms of his father's will or his conspicuous absence from it. He accepted the sisters' offer that they divide his father's cash—as opposed to real estate—four ways, and he soon left Mexico for good. Neither in his poems nor his prose did he ever mention his father again. But Hughes's mother was another case altogether.

The deaths of his parents freed Langston Hughes to become more fully his own man (and writer).

A Greater Loss

Carrie Mercer Hughes Clark led a difficult and troubled life. Twice married and twice divorced, she also changed residences many times. A person of substantial talent, Carrie was never able to capitalize upon it. She, therefore, trusted, hoped, and believed that her talented son would rescue her from poverty and shame. This was best seen in one of her letters on the subject:

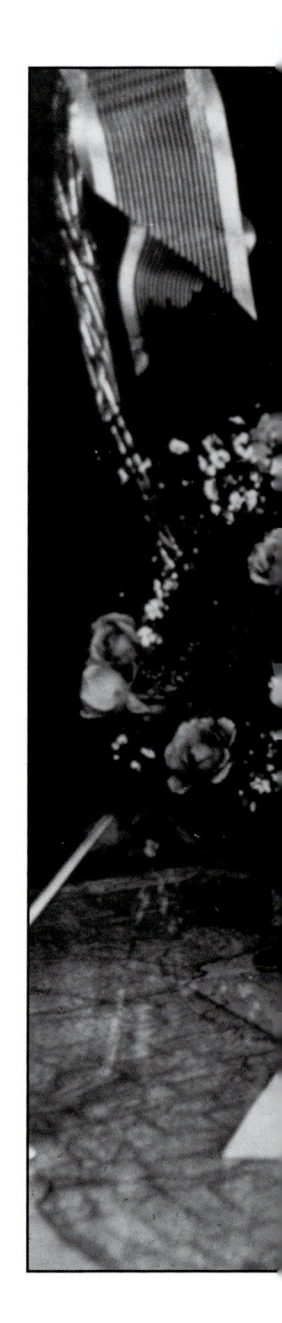

> My Dear Langston:
>
> I got your letter with both checks. Thank you very much…Now Langston, I want you to come see me. Are you coming here & when?
>
> How long will you stay!
>
> If you are not I won't pay rent here as I cannot stay here alone this winter. I just cannot. I am not well enough…Oh Langston, I do want you to come. Please answer return mail these questions.[1]

Hughes did all he could for his mother. His first book of poems, *The Weary Blues*, was dedicated to her. Time and again, Hughes ignored or shelved his own needs in order to help his mother.

Carrie Clark died of cancer in 1938. Langston Hughes arranged his mother's funeral and paid her remaining debts.

Though many Americans admired FDR, Hughes saw him as a man upholding systems of segregation and discrimination, including in the war effort.

Hughes and FDR

Like many African Americans, Langston Hughes admired Eleanor Roosevelt. The American First Lady was everywhere during the 1930s, uplifting and encouraging all Americans—including black citizens, who encountered much oppression in American society. But Hughes did not admire, or particularly like, President Franklin D. Roosevelt. He saw FDR as the protector of a system rich in injustice to his fellow people. Hughes was also one of the first to speak out against the incarceration of Japanese Americans when World War II began.

Though he experienced sadness, Hughes also felt free. Charlotte Mason had once been "Godmother," but her demands had limited his expression. With both of his parents gone, he was free to be his own man, and nowhere was this better expressed than in his poetry. Hughes had need of his poetic gift. The Second World War would change everything.

War and Protest

Adolf Hitler's invasion of Poland in September 1939 launched the Second World War. Though Hughes was thirty-eight, there was still a possibility he would be drafted. The last thing Hughes wanted was to fight in a war that he viewed as merely a contest between greater and lesser evils. He had absolutely no admiration for Nazi Germany, but he did not wish to die in the service of the United States, a deeply flawed nation still mired in oppression of black men and women.

Hughes's conflict revolved around Jim Crow, the name for the social and economic system that kept black Americans second-class citizens in their own country. Hughes's life in Harlem was sometimes wonderful and often pleasant, but he was all too aware of the injustice suffered by African Americans in the southern states. On top of all the other indignities was the simple fact that the US Army and Navy were still segregated. Black soldiers fought in all-black units. Enraged by this continued and blatant racism, Hughes wrote one of his most unpopular poems, "Comment on War."

> Let us kill off youth.
> For the sake of *truth*.
>
> We who are old know what truth is—
> Truth is a bundle of vicious lies
> Ties together and sterilized--
> A war-maker's bait for unwise youth
> To kill off each other
> For the sake of
> *Truth*.[2]

Hughes wrote this poem before America entered World War II, but nonetheless it highlights the kind of discrimination that endured well into that Second World War and beyond. Throughout World War II, Hughes performed a balancing act: he read poems aloud to large

Even as they prepared to make the ultimate sacrifice for the United States, black Americans were still segregated in the military during World War II.

groups of soldiers; he spoke up for the war effort; but at the same time, he derided the society that maintained Jim Crow. Hughes usually saved his anger for private letters, such as the one to his friend Noel Sullivan:

> The position of Negro troops training in the South—many Northern boys who have never been used to such severe and irrational Jim Crow—is very dangerous, so soldiers returning on furloughs say. It seems the lower Southern elements resent colored boys in uniform and go out of their way often to be rude and unpleasant. This added to the Jim Crow cars and lack of service in diners send the Negro boys back North much madder at the South than they should be at Hitler.[3]

Simple

Though he was full of political zeal and righteous anger, Hughes, like many poets, was still able to keep the beauty of the everyday close to his heart. In 1943, Hughes introduced his most long-lasting character: Jesse B. Semple, otherwise known as "Simple." As Hughes describes it, he came up with the idea for Simple through a conversation with a black couple at a local bar. The lady asked penetrating and important questions while the man gave simple answers. Though Hughes may have colored that evening with rose-covered glasses, he did love the nightlife and very likely found much of value there, including ordinary conversations between lovers.

By this time, Hughes already had a syndicated column in the *Chicago Defender*, a primarily African American newspaper. He now introduced Simple to the audience and

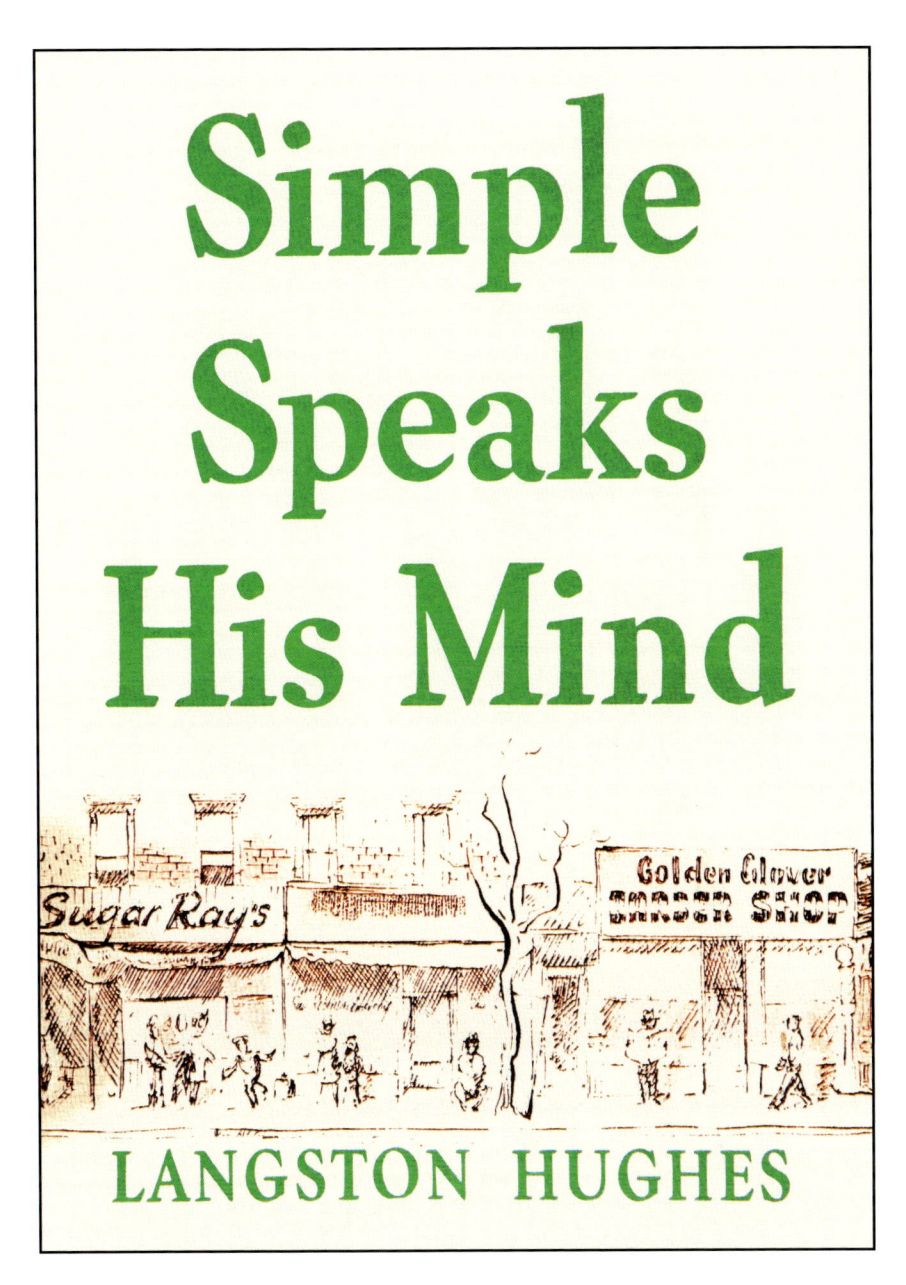

The "Simple" stories, originally published in Hughes's column in the *Chicago Defender*, captured the ironic beauty of everyday encounters.

entertained readers for the next fifteen years with charming tales of seemingly ordinary encounters, often moving in their simplicity. Of course, Simple was not as simple as he sounds. At times, Hughes's words, delivered from Simple's mouth, sounded truly profound:

> "Look here at these headlines, man, where Congress is busy passing laws. While they're making all these laws, it looks like to me they ought to make one setting up a few Game Preserves for Negroes."

> "What ever gave you that fantastic idea?" I asked.

> "A movie short I saw the other night," said Simple, "about how the government is protecting wild life, preserving fish and game, and setting aside big tracts of land where nobody can fish, hoot, hunt, nor harm a single living creature with furs, fins, or feathers. But it did not show a thing about Negroes."[4]

As one might expect, Hughes's sharp insight and sharper tongue irritated many white readers. While some admired Langston Hughes during the 1920s and "tolerated" him during the 1930s, for some this was a turning point: they wrote him off, declaring he had nothing left to say. Those thin-skinned readers could not have been more mistaken. Hughes and Simple had plenty more to say.

Thanks to Simple, Hughes became known to the great majority of African American readers. His regular column in the *Chicago Defender* made him one of the leading voices of the black community. But white readers generally did not subscribe to the *Defender,* and they regarded Hughes as a throwback, a person whose words had once rung with certainty but now lacked conviction. The great irony was that the leading black poet had become a major writer of prose and he still did not receive the respect he deserved. But Hughes would have the last laugh.

Man of Letters

By 1950, Langston Hughes had firmly established himself as a leading spokesperson for African Americans. Whether through gentle wit or biting sarcasm, he wrote the words echoed by millions of others.

A Settled Home

Hughes was finally settled in one place. His dear friends Emerson and Toy Harper practically adopted him, and he lived in their apartment building in Harlem for the rest of his life. With a fixed home, Hughes was able to spread his literary net even wider, and he embarked on a period that most authors can only look on with admiration or envy.

As early as 1935, Hughes did some writing for the theatre, hoping to make in Hollywood the money he had failed to find in New York City. He kept at it during the 1940s and found much success in the 1950s. Throughout this time, he continued to write his column for the *Chicago Defender*.

Though he lived in this Harlem apartment building the rest of his life, Langston Hughes continued to look—and act—the part of the wanderer.

Friends, fans, and admirers were often puzzled by Hughes. How could he be so utterly charming and easygoing, yet live alone, they asked? And how did he succeed in tackling the mountain of work he took on? One of the best answers is provided by the writer Milton Meltzer, who collaborated with Hughes on two books:

> He poured coffee, pushing aside the pile of unread mail that had arrived that morning…The never-absent cigarette dangled from his lip, the ashes tumbling down over his shirt as he talked. Getting up, he pulled together several folders lying about on shelves or the desk…It was a terrifying mountain of work to think of attacking. Didn't he ever intend to take it easy? Not hardly, he said. He hoped to be writing for a long time. He liked it, and thought he was lucky to be able to make a living from something he liked doing.[1]

Throughout life, Langston Hughes worked very hard. He did not kid himself: his ambition was to be a writer and a great one. Part of Hughes's personal magic, however, part of what kept him going—year after year and book after book—was his sense of play. For Hughes, writing was a good business—a good line of work—but not a deadly serious one. Time and again, younger poets and prose writers came away from meeting Hughes with a sense of wonder—here was an older man who had not lost the magic of youth.

Under Suspicion

One thing Langston Hughes did not anticipate was suspicion on the part of the federal government. He had

In 1953, Hughes faced accusations of Communist sympathies and was called to testitfy before the House Un-American Activities Committee.

been a good citizen his entire life, paying his taxes and urging African Americans to give their best during World War II, even though he resented Jim Crow. But Hughes had traveled so much that he came under suspicion during the McCarthy era of the early 1950s. Hughes was suspected of having communist sympathies. The "evidence" was ample. One had only to look back to the 1930s, when he traveled to the Soviet Union, and the 1940s, when he wrote unflattering poems about the US military. In the highly charged political climate of the "Red Scare" of the 1950s, this was enough to suggest that Hughes was a communist and, thus, a threat to American security. Many artists from all creative fields were accused of having communist sympathies, and the fallout was often disastrous: several men and women found themselves blacklisted from their respective industries, unable to find work.

Alert to the high stakes, Hughes immediately accepted the challenge. He agreed to testify before the House Un-American Activities Committee. Much of Hughes's testimony was worked out in advance. On the stand, he admitted to having admired aspects of Soviet Russian society but declared he had never formally joined the Community Party or any similar group. The investigators did not have it in for Hughes; they regarded his testimony as crucial to building their case against other suspects. Hughes's testimony was well attended and documented, but he soon left the witness stand and was not recalled. He had narrowly escaped a fate that would have almost certainly ended his career and tarnished his legacy.

Chapter 1

A Dream Realized

Throughout life, Langston Hughes struggled with himself. Though he appeared easygoing, even "simple," he was anything but. By nature, he craved company; by virtue of his work, he needed a measure of solitude. And though he rejected both his father and his advice about getting up and getting on in the world, Langston did suffer some of the same compulsive drive. The only thing he had not done during his sixty-odd years was to "do nothing." One final triumph remained.

Black Nativity

Ever since the mid-1930s, Hughes had dabbled with writing for the stage. He never enjoyed it as much as writing poetry, but the pay—while not marvelous—was usually better. Hughes either penned or assisted in the writing of several plays, but it was *Black Nativity*, a gospel scene set in a modern slum, that won him great applause. It opened on Broadway in December 1961, and critics practically tripped over each other in their eagerness to pay it high tribute. Once again,

Hughes's *Black Nativity* was adapted into a film starring Forest Whitaker and Angela Bassett in 2013.

Hughes had hit the nail squarely on the head.

Black Nativity earned Hughes more than any of his previous literary efforts, but even now he was not out of the woods. For Hughes, the early 1960s represented more of the same, in that he wrote furiously, both to make a living and to satisfy his internal drive. To be sure, he could not—and did not—ignore the important social changes that sprang up in those years.

The Fight for Civil Rights

When Hughes was a teenager, and even in his twenties, the idea of desegregation and something even approaching racial equality seemed a dream. Thanks to his literary talent, Hughes had avoided some of the worst situations that an African American male could experience. Even so, it was not until the early 1960s that he witnessed some positive, effectual change.

While Hughes was not acquainted with Malcolm X or close friends with Reverend Martin Luther King Jr., his poems rendering the reality of the black experience in

Hughes met President John F. Kennedy in 1961 when he was invited to a luncheon in honor of Léopold Sédar Sengho, a poet and then-president of Senegal.

America served as inspiration for protesters and activists around the country.

Though he seldom participated in protest marches, Hughes did have the opportunity to meet with major leaders. In 1961, he was a member of a delegation of literary figures that met with President John F. Kennedy at the White House. And in 1966, he was one of the leaders of a United States delegation to Senegal, Africa.

When friends asked if he would ever slow down, Hughes usually gave the same answer. He chuckled and said he could not afford to. There was truth to that statement. Thanks to his liberal friendship and hospitality, and because he spent so much time helping younger writers, Hughes was still in difficult financial shape. Just as he began pulling out of that difficulty, Hughes's health started to give way.

Though he lived in Harlem, quite close to some of the best physicians in the world, Hughes had no doctor and remained close-mouthed about his health. Slim and athletic in youth, the weight gain he experienced in his sixties took a toll on his health. It was while on vacation in Greece that Hughes's physical limitations—and their effect on his hobbies—became noticeable: the once eager tourist and enthusiast sat out many of the most enjoyable parts of the tour. Even so, Hughes's death came as nearly a complete surprise to the literary community.

The Passing of a Poet

Hughes died on May 20, 1967. He had been hospitalized a week earlier, and doctors believed there was a chance to save him. But years of high blood pressure had taken their

Langston Hughes remains a titan in the field of poetry and an emblem of the cultural contributions of the Harlem Renaissance.

toll, and Hughes passed away at the hospital, with only a few close friends aware of his condition.

Some were critical of Hughes's career, even in death and as they praised his potential. *The Nation* critic wrote that "As a poet, he did not really improve. Of the twenty poems judged to be Hughes' best in James A. Emanuel's useful critical study, Langston Hughes—in which readers will find most of their favorites—all but six were written in the twenties. One could trace developments in Hughes' poetry—his development from blues to bop rhythms, for example, but not artistic growth."[1] The *New York Times* ran a front-page obituary. The *Times* recounted many of Hughes's accomplishments, commenting that "whenever Mr. Hughes had a pencil and paper in his hands, he would scribble poetry."[2] The most revealing aspect of the article came when Hughes was quoted as saying, "My writing has been largely concerned with the depicting of Negro life in America."[3]

Perhaps there were some readers who were unaware of Hughes up to this point, but very likely 9 out of 10 knew that Hughes was a person dedicated and devoted to improving the lives of common African Americans. Deep down, Hughes was despondent in his final years. Though he appreciated and applauded the efforts of Martin Luther King and others, Hughes did not believe white Americans' beliefs about their black neighbors would be changed. Though Hughes was seldom friendly with W. E. B. Du Bois (the two were like night and day, where personality is concerned), he was closer, in his last weeks and months to Du Bois's spirit than to that of the new civil rights leaders.

Hughes's final poem, published in *The Crisis* a year after his death, suggests his melancholy:

> On the shoals of Nowhere,
> Cast up—my boat,
> Bow all broken,
> No longer afloat.
>
> On the shoals of Nowhere,
> Wasted—my song—
> Yet taken by the sea wind
> And blown along.[4]

A simple reading of this poem, "Flotsam," suggests Hughes is in the depths of despair, that he believes his work has been for naught. But this type of reading ignores the rich humor and optimism that Hughes employed throughout life. For the millions who have been touched by Hughes's work, he remains the small-town boy who made good, the stepchild of a regal African American family who persevered despite all manner of obstacles. His boat was cast up and its bow was broken, but the sea wind would carry his message.

Chronology

1901

Langston Hughes is born in Joplin, Missouri.

Topeka newspaper reports Hughes and his mother on their way to Buffalo, NY.

1906

Hughes and his mother go to Mexico to visit his father.

1914

Hughes's maternal grandmother dies.

1915

Hughes enters high school in Cleveland, Ohio.

1919

He goes to Mexico with his father.

1920

He goes to Mexico alone. On the train trip, he pens "Rivers."

1921

Hughes enters Columbia University.

1922

Hughes takes a ship up the Hudson River.

1923

He takes a freighter to Africa.

1924

Hughes returns to Harlem after time spent in France and Italy.

1925
The Weary Blues is published in the same year that Countee Cullen's *Color* is published.

1926
Hughes pens "The Negro Artist and the Racial Mountain" for *The Nation*.

1927
He meets "Godmother" Charlotte Mason, and she becomes his patron.

1930
Hughes breaks with "Godmother" Mason.

1936
Hughes's father dies in Mexico.

1937-1938
Hughes goes to Spain as part of the International Brigade.

1938
Hughes's mother dies in New York City.

1942
Hughes invents "Simple" in his weekly newspaper column.

1946
Hughes writes a touching tribute to his old friend Countee Cullen.

1951
Hughes is questioned by the federal government for communist sympathies.

1961

Black Nativity opens in New York City.

1966

Hughes travels to Senegal.

1967

Hughes dies in New York City.

Chapter Notes

Chapter 1
Kinship and Kingship
1. *The Plaindealer* (Topeka, KS), May 17, 1901, p. 3.
2. *The Plaindealer*, December 20, 1901, p. 2.

Chapter 2
Poems of the Oppressed
1. Arnold Rampersad and David Roessel, eds., *The Collected Poems of Langston Hughes* (New York, NY: Vintage Classics, 1994), p. 30.
2. Langston Hughes, *The Big Sea: An Autobiography* (New York, NY: Hill and Wang, 1940), p. 29.
3. Hughes, p. 30.
4. Hughes, p. 37.

Chapter 3
Rivers and Oceans
1. Langston Hughes, *The Big Sea: An Autobiography* (New York, NY: Hill and Wang, 1940), p. 29.
2. "The Negro Speaks of Rivers," *The Crisis*, June 1921, p. 71.
3. Hughes, p. 32.

Chapter 4
Student and Sailor
1. Langston Hughes, *The Big Sea: An Autobiography* (New York, NY: Hill and Wang, 1940), p. 103.
2. Arnold Rampersad and David Roessel, eds., *Selected Letters of Langston Hughes* (New York, NY: Alfred A. Knopf, 2015), p. 28–29.
3. Rampersad, p. 31.

Chapter 5
Sudden Fame

1. Langston Hughes, *The Weary Blues* (New York, NY: Knopf, 1926), p. 5.
2. Hughes, p. 82.
3. Hughes, p. 57.
4. Langston Hughes, "The Negro Artist and the Racial Mountain," *The Nation*, June 23, 1926.
5. Ibid.
6. Ibid.

Chapter 6
The Godmother

1. Arnold Rampersad and David Roessel, eds., *The Collected Poems of Langston Hughes* (New York, NY: Vintage Classics, 1994), p. 212.

Chapter 7
Russia and Spain

1. Arnold Rampersad and David Roessel, eds., *The Collected Poems of Langston Hughes* (New York, NY: Vintage Classics, 1994), p. 138.

Chapter 8
Simply Himself

1. Carmaletta M. Williams and John Edgar Tidwell, eds., *My Dear Boy: Carrie Hughes's Letters to Langston Hughes, 1926–1938* (Athens, GA: University of Georgia Press, 2013), pp. 78–79.
2. Langston Hughes, "Comment on War," *The Crisis*, June 1940, p. 190.
3. Arnold Rampersad and David Roessel, eds., *Selected Letters of Langston Hughes* (New York: Alfred A. Knopf, 2015), p. 244.

4. Donna Akiba Sullivan Harper, *Not So Simple: The "Simple" Stories by Langston Hughes* (Columbia, MO: University of Missouri Press, 1995), pp. 53–54.

Chapter 9
Man of Letters

1. Milton Meltzer, *Langston Hughes: A Biography* (New York, NY: Thomas Y. Crowell, 1968), pp. xii-xiii.

Chapter 10
A Dream Realized

1. Tish Dace, ed., *Langston Hughes: The Contemporary Reviews* (New York, NY: Cambridge University Press, 1997), pp. 709–710.
2. "Langston Hughes, Writer, 65, Dead," *New York Times*, May 23, 1967, p. 1.
3. *New York Times*, p. 47.
4. "Flotsam," *The Crisis*, June 1968, p. 194.

Glossary

caricature A broad rendering or representation of something or someone.

Communism A political belief system that supports the idea that people should be paid for work based upon their needs and abilities.

institutional racism Racial discrimination that becomes a part of society through habit and practice, not through law.

interloper A stranger or intruder.

internalize To take an idea, usually harmful to oneself, and integrate it into one's thoughts and beliefs.

laurels Praise for one's accomplishments.

loggerheads In conflict with one another.

patron A person who supports artists by financing their projects and lives.

peripatetic Wandering from place to place, without a permanent home.

philanthropic Generous, trying to do good in the world, usually through financial contributions.

punctilious Extremely focused on details and proper behavior.

Red Scare A period in the 1950s where men and women were often accused of being Communists, which came with the danger of being blackballed from their industries or professions.

schism A break between people or groups.

wanderlust A desire to travel or see the world.

Further Reading

BOOKS

Hughes, Langston. *The Big Sea: An Autobiography*. New York, NY: Hill and Wang, 1940.

Rampersad, Arnold, and David Roessel, eds. *The Collected Poems of Langston Hughes*. New York, NY: Vintage Classics, 1994.

Rampersad, Arnold, and David Roessel, eds. *Selected Letters of Langston Hughes*. New York, NY: Alfred A. Knopf, 2015.

Stabler, David. *Kid Authors: True Tales of Childhood from Famous Authors*. Philadelphia, PA: Quirk Books, 2018.

WEBSITES

Langston Hughes – Biography
https://www.biography.com/video/langston-hughes-mini-biography-2174109638
A short video biography of Langston Hughes.

Langston Hughes – Poetry Foundation
https://www.poetryfoundation.org/poets/langston-hughes
An overview of Langston Hughes's career and life.

Langston Hughes Society
http://www.langstonhughessociety.org
A scholarly society dedicated to the works of Langston Hughes.

Index

**Charlotte
Etinde-Crompton**

**Samuel
Willard Crompton**

About the Authors

Charlotte Etinde-Crompton was born and raised in Zaire and came to Massachusetts at the age of twenty. Her artistic sensibility stems from her early exposure to the many talented artists of her family and tribe, which included master wood-carvers. Her interest in African American art has been an abiding passion since her arrival in the United States.

Samuel Willard Crompton is a tenth-generation New Englander who now lives in metropolitan Atlanta. For twenty-eight years, he was a professor of history at Holyoke Community College. His early interest in the arts comes from his wood-carver father and his oil-painter mother. Crompton is the author and editor of many books, including a number of nonfiction young adult titles with Enslow Publishing. This is his first collaboration with his wife.